POLITE SATIRES

POLITE SATIRES
By CLIFFORD BAX

Containing
THE UNKNOWN HAND, THE VOLCANIC ISLAND
SQUARE PEGS

One-Act Play Reprint Series

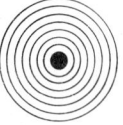
Core Collection Books, inc.
GREAT NECK, NEW YORK

First Published 1922
Reprinted 1976

PR
6003
.A987
P6
1976

International Standard Book Number
0-8486-2001-3

Library of Congress Catalog Number
76-40385

PRINTED IN THE UNITED STATES OF AMERICA

Contents

THE UNKNOWN HAND, 7

THE VOLCANIC ISLAND, 21

SQUARE PEGS, 35

THE UNKNOWN HAND

Characters

JULIET
HELEN

THE UNKNOWN HAND

SCENE. *A Room in* JULIET'S *Flat. Back centre, a fire. To its right, a chair ; to its left, an easy chair and a small table. Two envelopes and a new novel lie on the table.* JULIET *is seated in the easy chair, looking into the fire*

JULIET (*dreamily*). Hans Andersen, when he was old and frail,
   Said that his life had been a fairy-tale. . . . (*Looking up.*)
That's what mine is! Think of it—by a freak
Of Fortune to be famous in one week,
And with my first book! Would it have made quite
Such a commotion had I dared to write
Under my name? Who knows? But if you've penned
A merciless portrait of your dearest friend,
You simply can't avow it. And a book
That bears a man's name has a weightier look
Somehow. My novel! Why, it seems an age
Since last I gloated on the title-page. (*She takes up the novel from the table.*)
' The Strong Man's Library. Number Seventeen.
" Calypso and Her Loves," by Galahad Green.
Second Impression.' Then down there, quite small.
The modest publishers—Chapman and Hall.
       (*Turning to the envelopes on the table.*)
Oh, and they've sent me—Is it from Chapman? Yes—
Another batch of cuttings from the Press.
Quite a lot, too! I'll give them just a glance
Before I go to supper.
(*Taking the envelope which is on top, she extracts a number of Press cuttings, looks through them hastily and tosses them back on to the table one by one.*)
       ' True romance.'
W. J. Turner—' Shows a man's desire
To write for men. . . . Much promise.' J. C. Squire.—

'*At times like Gosse.* . . .' Who wrote that? Squire again,
But in a different paper—'*Stuff for men.* . . .
Gosse-like at moments.' Edward Shanks—'*No learner,
A finished craftsman.*' W. J. Turner—
'*Impressive.*' J. C. Squire.—'*His novel ranks
Among the best books of the season.* . . .' Shanks.—
'*Impressive.*' Shanks.—'*Almost the true Gosse fire.* . . .'
Turner again. '*A man's book.*' J. C. Squire.—
My poor head swims! How very queer to find
Ten papers, three reviewers and one mind.
They're like the Isle of Man. Suppose I beg
Prettily? Would they make me their fourth leg?
Here's praise enough. Indeed, you'd think I knew them—
Or that they hoped I might in turn review them.
    (*Looking again at the table, she picks up the second envelope.*)
And here? Oh, horror! Helen's writing—hers,
I'm sure, and what wild spluttering characters!
Their wildness might be due to haste, but not
The Maenad fury of that final blot.
She's read the book, and recognized with rage
The portrait of herself on every page,
In every line. She couldn't miss it. Why
Didn't I make Calypso small and shy,
Dark and not fair? Whatever made me draw
Helen complete, even to her slightest flaw?
Everything's there—green eyes, the Chelsea flat,
The craze for Morny bath-salts, even that! . . .
I let Calypso live at such a pace
Too, that I daren't look Helen in the face,
I simply daren't. But stay! She might have seen
The book: she can't think I am Galahad Green.
There's hope. I'll soon see what she has to say . . (*She opens the letter.*)
'My dearest Juliet'—'dearest,' anyway!—

THE UNKNOWN HAND

' I'm furious, but I shan't say what about
Until we meet. Promise you won't be out
This evening. I shall call at eight o'clock.
Helen.' At least her letter saves the shock
Of meeting unprepared, and I'll be able
To sweep these wretched cuttings from the table
What *is* the time? Exactly eight. Oh dear,
At any minute now she may be here
Storming my ears off. What a risk I took!
And then—she's just the girl to read a book,
Find her own portrait there, done all too well,
And taxi-ing to the publishers pell-mell
Demand to have the author's home-address.
Chapman and Hall, however great their stress,
Would never give it, would they? When we met
Their manager seemed such a perfect pet . . .
     (*A bell rings. Noise outside.*)
 There she is.
    (HELEN *rushes in—still wearing her furs.*)
HELEN (*dramatically*). Juliet!
JULIET. Well, what's wrong, my dear?
HELEN. Nothing—at least—I *am* so glad you're here
    (*She takes both of* JULIET'*s hands.*)
JULIET. I read your letter just in time. The fact
 Is that it caught me in the very act
 Of going out to supper.
HELEN. But you'll stay
 Now? It's important—what I've come to say—
 And yet so horrible that I've scarce the heart
 To speak of it. I don't know how to start.
JULIET. I guess. You've jilted John! I always said
 You would. Or has he jilted you instead?

THE UNKNOWN HAND

HELEN (*breaking*). Oh, don't be flippant, Juliet. Can't you see
   It's not a laughing matter? Should I be
   In such a state about a love-affair?
   I'm not pre-Shaw.

JULIET.   Then why——

HELEN.   As if I'd care
   Because John tried to leave me. He'll as soon
   Do that as find an oil-field in the moon.
   No—this is something serious.

JULIET.   Won't you take
   Your furs off, and sit down?

HELEN.   For goodness' sake
   Don't vex me with that calm superior tone!
   Once you were sympathetic, but you've grown
   More and more selfish every month. Of late
   I've hardly seen you. *Now* I come here straight
   From being insulted, being driven half-mad,
   By some sly undiscoverable cad,
   And there you sit, impassive and content,
   Like Middle-Age upon a monument
   Smiling at grief.

JULIET.   I don't flare up like you,
   Helen. But wait! I've been insulted, too.

HELEN. Really? But listen! If I keep it back
   A minute more, it means a nerve-attack.
   Juliet—I've read a book——

JULIET.   A novel?

HELEN.   Yes—
   A new one. But however did you guess?
   It's only just out.

THE UNKNOWN HAND

JULIET.   Surely you can't mean——
HELEN (*holding up a copy*). 'Calypso and Her Loves'!
JULIET (*doing likewise*).   By Galahad Green!
  Now, that's extraordinary—the very same!
HELEN. You've read it? Oh, it makes me blush for shame.
JULIET. Stick by me—even now. I know you will.
HELEN. What? I? Dear Juliet, you can love me still!
JULIET. To see them set down—all one's little tricks . . .
HELEN. To have one's soul supplied at eight-and-six . . .
JULIET. Or hired from Mudie's, read by every clerk—
HELEN. And every sniggering waitress after dark.
JULIET. I could have stood a mere divorce. But this!
HELEN. Every one *must* know who Calypso is.
JULIET. Of course. I simply daren't be seen about.
HELEN. Who *is* this Galahad Green? I can't find out.
JULIET. A blood-sucker, a literary flea!
HELEN. I'll sue the cad for libel. Just you see!
JULIET. You dear! It ought to be *my* action, though.
HELEN. Yours? You can't mind as much as I, you know.
JULIET. Can't I! You think I'd stay in England now?
HELEN. What? Leave your home? No, that I can't allow.
JULIET. Won't you come, too? To-morrow I shall start.
HELEN. Of course you're sweet to take it so to heart—
JULIET. Who wouldn't—with her reputation gone?
HELEN. It must be such a bitter pill for John!
JULIET. What would John care because I'm painted black?
HELEN. You?

13

JULIET.   In this book, this dastardly attack—
  Yet, you dear noble girl, at least it's shown
  That to you my misfortunes are your own.
HELEN. Juliet—what *do* you mean? Sometimes your gibes
  Are most ill-timed. You know the book describes
  Me.
JULIET. You're not serious?
HELEN.   I? Of course I am . . .
  And now that I've discovered what a sham
  You were with all your sympathy, I could hurl
  The foul book at your head. You heartless girl!
  Is this a time to mock me, to pretend
  You care so much about your slandered friend
  That you won't stay in England? If that's your
  Notion of fun, it isn't mine, be sure.
JULIET. I wasn't being funny—not a bit,
  Really. It's simply that the cap does fit—
  I *am* Calypso!
HELEN.   Well, I never heard
  Such nonsense in my life. It's too absurd.
  Oh, if I could but think that one or two
  Readers might fancy it was meant for you,
  I'd take some pleasure in my life again,
  Dance, have a feast of oysters and champagne,
  Buy a new winter frock and hat, instead
  Of wishing, as I do, that I were dead.
  For you deserve it—you that make a joke
  Out of my misery.
JULIET.   Helen—when I spoke
  Of being Calypso, didn't I, to my shame,
  Own the wild sins that cluster round her name?
  Alas, I meant it.

THE UNKNOWN HAND

HELEN.   Nobody could be
So blind as not to know it's me—I—me:
And since you're now my enemy, I shall go
At once. But after this, I'd have you know,
Our friendship's dead—for always! Please forget
You ever knew me.
JULIET.   Helen, don't go yet . .
HELEN. I must. And let me say that if you call
To-morrow you'll have wasted time, that's all.
I shan't go home to-night.
JULIET.   Where will you sleep?
HELEN. Battersea Bridge is high, and the Thames deep.
JULIET. You wicked child! You mustn't talk like that.
HELEN. A plunge and then——
JULIET.   With such a pretty hat?
HELEN *(returning)*. You never said you liked it.
JULIET.   No. I've been
So worried all day by this Galahad Green.
For really, Helen, once and for all be certain
It's not from *your* life that he's wrenched the curtain.
You can still face the world. You've not the least
Cause to abominate the loathsome beast—
Except as I'm your friend: and since I know,
Now, that your strange mistake has hurt you so,
Believe me, I rejoice—yes, even rejoice—
That I, not you, suffer by Galahad's choice.
I bear it willingly. Must I prove my case?
Give me one moment, while I find the place . .
   (She opens the book and searches through it feverishly.)
HELEN *(opening copy)*. Oh, if it comes to evidence . . . ! But indeed
I simply can't go through it!

THE UNKNOWN HAND

JULIET.   Let me read
  Page twenty-four: 'Between him and his wife
  A deep gulf lay. She wanted to see life
  Through her own eyes, but he preferred, she knew,
  The monocle of *The Saturday Review*'—
  There! Don't you see? That paper's just the one
  I always said would patronize the sun.

HELEN. That? Why, look here—page forty-two—'Her eyes
  Were green, her honey-coloured——'

JULIET.   Mere disguise!
  He *had* to change a little here and there.
  Listen: 'She glowered——'

HELEN.   'Her honey-coloured hair
  Lay in profusion on her shoulders——'

JULIET.   'Then
  She thought "It's time——"

HELEN.   'To win the love of men—
  'What's that?' she cried. 'I ever hated sin——'

JULIET. "But now I'll change. To-morrow I'll begin . . .
  My sins are many. Can they be washed away?"'

HELEN. 'So she used Morny bath-salts every day.
  Often she'd sponge herself for hours, and dream
  Of love, veiled only by the bashful steam.
  Sometimes, perhaps, an over-amorous drop
  Would trickle down——'

JULIET (*shocked*).   Helen, my dear—do stop!
  Really!

HELEN. But that's conclusive!

JULIET.   I admit
  That she had beauty, savoir-faire, and wit,
  But she was wicked, too, reckless and haughty——

THE UNKNOWN HAND

HELEN. I can't pretend that I was never naughty.

JULIET. Naughty, perhaps; but you could never trip so
Continually as Mr. Green's Calypso.

HELEN. I do believe you think I wouldn't dare
Calypso's deeds. I've done them all—so there!

JULIET. Well, you shall have the truth. I'll make a clean
Breast of it. Who, you ask, is Galahad Green?
I know him!

HELEN. Juliet! And he dares affirm
That I was not. . . . The lily-livered worm!

JULIET. But if he writes a letter to the Press
Declaring that he never saw you——

HELEN. Yes,
And makes me look a fool. What can I do
When every one I meet says 'Is it you . . .
That wicked gorgeous creature, that wild thing
Ecstatic and unmoral as the Spring . . .?'
Of course I owned it.

JULIET. Helen—I can still
Save you. I'll make him write——

HELEN No, no!

JULIET. I will—
And now, at once. The telephone!

HELEN (*stopping* JULIET). But I say
You're not to!

JULIET (*struggling*). Let me go! We can't delay.

HELEN. Juliet, for goodness' sake don't be so dense!

JULIET. What *do* you mean?

THE UNKNOWN HAND

HELEN. Where's your intelligence,
　Your tact, your feminine intuition? Where
　Your sympathy? Must I lay my soul quite bare?

JULIET *(returning and collapsing into her chair)*. So far as I'm concerned
　you're talking Greek.

HELEN. They've sold nine thousand copies in one week.

JULIET. Why, one would think, in spite of all that's passed,
　You liked the book.

HELEN. So you've got there at last!
　You *are* an also-ran.

JULIET. Good heavens!

HELEN. I had
　To *say* that I was furious, and not glad;
　But what girl wouldn't feel some little stir
　Of pride when all the town's in love with her?
　You don't know half that's happened. This new novel
　Has simply made all other writers grovel.
　Bennett's gone mad with envy. J. C. Snaith
　Is in decline. Galsworthy's a mere wraith.
　Chesterton, having burnt his cap and bells,
　Drowned himself in a butt of Malmesey. Wells
　Vowed to the Press he'd never write again.
　May Sinclair, Violet Hunt, and Clemence Dane
　Have gone—forevermore to breathe the air
　Of Iceland. Poor Hugh Walpole's in despair.
　Now do you see my point? Didn't you lie
　When you said that Calypso wasn't I?

JULIET. Yes.

HELEN. And the author learnt it all from you.
　I think you owe me something.

JULIET. Very true . .
　What do you want?

THE UNKNOWN HAND

HELEN. Oh, Juliet—since I've been
  His model, do you think that Mr. Green
  Would possibly—just some day—take me out
  To supper?
JULIET. When? To-night?
HELEN. Could he?
JULIET. No doubt.
HELEN. Let's ring him up.
JULIET (*stopping her*). Who said that *I* was dense?
HELEN. But if he's free——?
JULIET. Use your intelligence,
  Your feminine intuition.
HELEN. Yes, but how?
JULIET. Galahad does invite you here and now.
  All is not masculine that's Green.
HELEN (*collapsing*). Your book!
JULIET. Here are my notices, if you care to look.
HELEN. My dear! . . . And all those famous novelists, too—
  Just shrivelling up with jealousy of *you*!
JULIET. Ah, but the poets! They are delighted—they
  Whose rustic hearts envy could never sway.
  Read what they've said.
HELEN. I'm sure it's very sweet.
  But somehow I can never keep my seat
  On Pegasus.
JULIET. Pegasus! No one rides *him* now:
  But ah, how steadily up Parnassus' brow,
  With farmyard straw, not vine-leaves, in his hair,
  Squire Turner Pounds on Shanks's de la Mare!

                                          1922.

THE
VOLCANIC ISLAND

Characters

DOROTHEA WYLDE
DOROTHY WILD

TO OLGA KATZIN

THE VOLCANIC ISLAND

SCENE. *The sitting-room of a flat in Knightsbridge. Back: centre, a fireplace with fire burning; right, a cupboard containing tea things; left, a tall lacquered screen. Front: a table on which are illustrated papers and a parcel of books tied with string; a chair to each side of the table.*
The outside door is heard closing.

DOROTHEA (*without*). Kate!
   (*She enters, right, in a fashionable Spring walking costume.*)
So I've caught her! Gone at half-past three—
   Gone to 'the pictures' with her young man Bill.
I hope she'll not be foolish. . . . Now for tea.
   (*She puts a kettle on the fire and brings a plate of cakes to the table.*)
   Ah! So the Mudie books have come—but still
Nothing from James. He really is *too* shy—
   And Mother always whispers when we meet,
'Well, dear, no startling news?' I wish he'd try!
   What have they sent me from New Oxford Street?
'Poems,' by Marshlight. . . . Quite a charming face. . . .
   Four portraits! . . . And how good it is to find
A note that tells the very hour and place
   When each mouse-lyric shook that mountain mind! . . .
And here? Oh Mudie! Sending *this* to *me*!
   'A Bed of Roses. George . . .' I'll try again. . . .
'Peeled Onions'! Now, whatever might *they* be?
   Of course! New tales by Ethel Colburn Mayne.
How hypodermic! What she does without!
   What whittling of mere obvious fact! Indeed
I sometimes tremble when her books come out
   For fear there won't be any words to read . . .
The last two? These—hobnobbing all this time,
   Not rent to rags, not mutually destroyed?

THE VOLCANIC ISLAND

For here's that famous work, ' Soul from the Slime,'
  By Jung, and here ' Slime from the Soul,' by Freud.
They may be *risqué* but how up to date—
  And James need never know I've read them. . . . Stop!
Surely? It is! A telegram! Oh, Kate,
  You little fool, to dump the books on top!
Reply paid, too . . . (*Reading*) ' Wylde, 15 Claridge Hill.
  Would you accept me for your husband? James . . .'
At last! . . What answer? If I say I will,
  The *Morning Post* will paragraph our names
With me as ' Dorothea, second child '—
  Et cetera—and *The Tatler*, I expect,
Will have a picture, ' Cupid's Bag. Miss Wylde,
  Sir James Adolphus Porter's bride-elect,
A well-known figure both where Fashion reigns
  And where our young intelligenzia meet. . . .'
But shall I? If he read more, had more brains,
  More fire, and just a little less conceit!

A VOICE (*behind the screen*). Marry him at your peril!

DOROTHEA (*not hearing*).   He's a man
  Of wealth and rank—an O.B.E.—and yet
To marry without love . . . Some people can.

THE VOICE.   I gave you honest warning. Don't forget!

DOROTHEA (*as before*). Most girls would jump at such an offer. Why
  Should I resent so much his pompous air,
His embonpoint?

THE VOICE.   It isn't you, but I!

DOROTHEA (*as before*). Or possibly, as Freud and Jung declare,
  Far under what we know ourselves to be
    Another self lies hidden. Am I, then——

THE VOICE. Like a volcanic island in the sea——

24

THE VOLCANIC ISLAND

DOROTHEA (*half hypnotized*). Of which no more is visible to men
   Than the mere summit—fair with azure light
     And flowers and birds and grain to sow and reap——

THE VOICE. While the huge base goes shelving out of sight
   To coral-caves and monsters of the deep.

DOROTHEA. How queer to think that while one part of me
   Is almost fond of James, another part
 Is—doubtful——

THE VOICE.   Doubtful? Just you wait and see!

DOROTHEA. Oh, for some ceremony, some magic art,
   To call up the subconscious mind!

THE VOICE.   Then hold
   Jung with your right hand, with your left hand Freud,
   And clap them thrice.

DOROTHEA (*following these directions*). Of course, I'm far too old . . .
   I ought to be more rationally employed . . .
 But still——

(DOROTHY WILD *darts out from behind the screen. She is a barbaric figure
   clad in furs and wearing a tiara of feathers.*)

DOROTHY.   O-hai! And so at last I'm free!

DOROTHEA (*recoiling*). Good gracious!

DOROTHY.   Don't you know me?

DOROTHEA.   What's your name?

DOROTHY. Dorothy Wild. You end yours with an 'e'
   And spell it with a 'y'—as though for shame
 Of owning sisterhood with trees and birds
   And dragonflies; as though you'd never run
 Beside the foam, shouting ecstatic words
   In the wind's ear, nor let the immortal sun

THE VOLCANIC ISLAND

    Have your whole body till Something, not of time,
        Like an elixir flowed through every vein.
    You? You lack pith. You'd never love through crime;
        But when *I* love, I dare—and brook no chain!
DOROTHEA. You're rather frightening. Still, do take a seat!
DOROTHY (*sitting on the table*). Chocolates! One for me?
DOROTHEA (*politely*).   Oh, not at all——
DOROTHY. Wild roses, love and chocolate—aren't they sweet?
DOROTHEA. Yes—well . . . I do hope nobody will call.
    We've not been introduced, but is it true
        That you're my own Subconscious?
DOROTHY.   There, you see
    The insolence of the Conscious! Part of you!
        Really! And why not you a part of me?
    How much of Time have *you* known? Twenty years;
        But I, whom not ten thousand can make old,
    Have worshipped trees, loved naiads, boxed the ears
        Of mountain satyrs, touched the Fleece of Gold,
    And ridden great centaurs. When I catch the strain
        Of Homer's verse I hear his very lyre
    Trembling: for me Hector is newly slain,
        And it was yesterday Troy fell in fire.
    They who at last have found me little guess
        Whither I lead. They fancy that one blow
    Has brought down Heaven in fragments. Nonetheless,
        I shall build what they think I overthrow!
    And you? You're just a weir that tames my power.
        I am the rushing car and you the brake
    That checks me: I the root and you the flower;
        I the true girl——
DOROTHEA.   Please try another cake.
    No doubt you're right, but Freud says——

THE VOLCANIC ISLAND

DOROTHY. Not a word
Against my good Columbus!

DOROTHEA. Hardly! Still,
I always thought from what I read and heard
That you were quite a monster.

DOROTHY. As you will,
I have my faults.

DOROTHEA. You do seem—shall I say
A trifle—crude?

DOROTHY. I'm what you'd like to be.

DOROTHEA. Oh, really! I'm not prim—I'm rather gay—
But that's no frock for going out to tea.
I *should* blush!

DOROTHY. Little hypocrite! Why, look—
What's that—oh you that have no eyes for men?

DOROTHEA. The 'Life of Gosse'—a very proper book.

DOROTHY. And underneath? La Vie Parisienne!
(Turning to the bookshelves.)
Then, here's Boccaccio, Havelock Ellis, too,
James Joyce rebound to look like Samuel Smiles,
Montaigne, Pierre Louys——

DOROTHEA. Any one but you
Would know I read them only for their styles.
I've stood enough. Please go!

DOROTHY. But where to go?
We two make up one girl.

DOROTHEA. Behind the screen.

DOROTHY. Not yet!

DOROTHEA. But I've important things——

DOROTHY.   I know—
   That's why I came. This telegram, you mean——
DOROTHEA. Mind your own business!
DOROTHY.   But it *is* mine, quite
   As much as yours. You'll take him? You insist?
   I won't!
DOROTHEA. How terrible! In this modern light
   Poor James looks almost like a bigamist. . . .
DOROTHY. Marry that hippopotamus if you dare!
DOROTHEA. Chairmen of Boards must be a little fat.
DOROTHY. James never rises but he 'takes' the chair.
DOROTHEA. He owns five cars, four houses, and a flat.
DOROTHY. Those and the seven deadly virtues, too.
DOROTHEA. He's forty-nine and never loved before.
DOROTHY. Why not? No girl would think of him but you.
DOROTHEA. A solid quiet man——
DOROTHY.   A solid bore!
DOROTHEA. Now, Dorothy, be reasonable. Sit down
   Like a well-mannered girl, or—if you must—
Crouch like a tigress there and fret and frown,
   But don't break in. I think it's only just
That I—for, after all, I really am
   The civilized and reputable Miss Wylde—
Should have the answering of this telegram.
   Say what you will, you're nothing but a child
Who lies among the daffodils of Spring,
   Lost in a book of marvels. At a glance
I know you—how you're dreaming of some king
   From over the blue mountains of romance

THE VOLCANIC ISLAND

Who'll set you on a charger black as night,
   And, spurring on by dragon-haunted caves,
Come to his castle just when the sunset-light
   In Fairyland floats on the girdling waves.
But kings aren't like that now. They puff cigars,
   Wear bowlers and check-suits, and fill the gaps
Left between opening Parliament and bazaars
   By betting on the racecourse. Or perhaps
You want some hero from a Conrad tale
   Who'd stand, white-ducked, against the torrid blue
And shoot down tribes with bullets fast as hail:
   But think, my dear—he simply wouldn't do.
Picture it. We should take him out to dine—
   The ladies would withdraw—he'd start to speak
About old Lingard, while they passed the wine,
   And go on with the story for a week.
No! We must have it clear. I much regret
   This violent tug-of-war between our aims
But—I'm determined.

DOROTHY.   Have you finished yet?
   Right. Then you can, but I won't, marry James.

DOROTHEA. Why not?

DOROTHY. Why not? Answer my questions. One:
   Does he beat time to music with his hand?

DOROTHEA. Well——

DOROTHY. Two: and talk of 'featuring,' 'Japs,' 'the Hun'?

DOROTHEA. Oh, sometimes——

DOROTHY.   Three: and does he understand
   That wicked frocks don't mean a wicked life?
     Four——

DOROTHEA. But, of course, there's no one perfect!

THE VOLCANIC ISLAND

DOROTHY.   Four:
  Wouldn't he read the golf news to his wife?
     Five: Can he tell—the next day—what you wore?
  Six: If he knows an author, will he wait
     To get a copy free or buy the book?
  Seven: Is he fond of curate stories? Eight:
     If, when you're dressed, you wonder how you look
  And ask him, as you're driving to the dance,
     Doesn't he, after everything you've done,
  Say ' Oh, all right '—without a single glance?
     Nine: If you flirt a little, for the fun
  Of being a woman, would he think you light?
     Ten: Does he say, when dining in Soho,
  ' I don't think we shall need champagne to-night—
     But if you really want it, let me know?'
  Eleven——

DOROTHEA. Oh please! I don't—in fact, I can't—
  Dispute the list. I'll openly admit
  That James is not the man I used to want. . . .

DOROTHY. Splendid! Now, where's his wire? We'll answer it
  With one majestic ' No.'

DOROTHEA (*stopping her*).   Not yet. Be kind!
  Think what I lose in losing James, and then
  You'll change your mind—your portion of our mind.
  I want a man to kiss——

DOROTHY.   But why not ten?

DOROTHEA. My dear! I want the life of modern man.
  I want to quote the works of Douglas Cole,
  Think all men base except the artisan,
     And smile at God, religion, and the soul.
  I want to find new genius everywhere.
     I want to sit in drawing-rooms and say

'Rossetti, Watts? Of course, they can't compare
   With Roger, or the smallest Fry, to-day.'
So, won't you be an angel? Share the flat
   In honourable retirement! Don't you see
You should?

DOROTHY.   Subconscious! Well, I may be that—
   But no great eras come apart from me.
What though to-day I have less power than you?
   The wheel will turn; and shall I not be there
To run with roses down Fifth Avenue
   And make a Roman revel in Mayfair?
No! I maintain my right to have a say
   In this, our marriage; therefore comprehend
Once and for all that I shall not give way!

DOROTHEA. I've done my best to treat you as a friend.
   You're just a little selfish pig! In fact,
   I don't know why you ever left your screen!

DOROTHY. I didn't come to argue but to act,
   And now I will!

DOROTHEA.   Whatever do you mean?

DOROTHY. I came to kill you.

DOROTHEA.   What?

DOROTHY.   You see this knife?
   The ghost of Caesar Borgia gave me this,
   And with it some advice on taking life.
   He only wished, he said, the chance were his!

DOROTHEA. But don't you know? One's not allowed to kill.

DOROTHY. Pooh! A mere whimsy of the Conscious Mind.
   Prepare!

DOROTHEA. But listen!

DOROTHY. No!

DOROTHEA. You can't!

DOROTHY. I will!
  Pray to the gods whom Freud has left behind!
  (DOROTHY *lunges with the knife at* DOROTHEA, *who escapes by darting to the left of the table. She raises her right hand high.*)

DOROTHEA. Stop! I pronounce on you this dreadful spell!
  Abracadabra: complex: transference:
  Theriomorphia—now it's working well—
  Father-imago: schizophrenia——

DOROTHY. Hence!
  Spare me!

DOROTHEA. Appendage-function: surrogate:
  Enantiodromia—doesn't that one hurt?—
  Libido: endopsychic——

DOROTHY. Wait, oh wait!

DOROTHEA. Persona: hypermnesia: extrovert! .
  Yield, in the holy names of Jung and Freud!

DOROTHY. I yield! I beg for nothing but fair play.

DOROTHEA. How?

DOROTHY. By a simple plan that would avoid
  All further wrangling.

DOROTHEA. Well, what is it?

DOROTHY. Say
  That you write half the telegram, and I
  The other half! That would be just.

DOROTHEA. Absurd!
  The first to write could give the whole reply.

THE VOLCANIC ISLAND

DOROTHY. A woman, and you don't want the last word? . . . Toss!

DOROTHEA (*producing a coin*). If you lose, you're not to call me names.

DOROTHY. Heads!

DOROTHEA. You *have* lost. Who is the better now? . . . 'Would you accept me for your husband.—James'— So runs the question, and the answer——

DOROTHY (*anxiously*).   How?

DOROTHEA. Read it!

DOROTHY (*in dismay*). 'Of course I would!'

DOROTHEA.   It's not so much
That I want James, as that you've made me cross.
In fact, if your behaviour had been such——

DOROTHY (*who, after a little puzzling is now in the act of writing*).

I'm glad to hear that you'll survive the loss.

DOROTHEA (*in slow horror*). You've spoilt it! Let me see! . . . 'Of course I would . . .
'Of course I would be damned first. . . .' Little cat!

DOROTHY. Don't be a silly child. As if you could
Abandon me for such a fool as that!
O Zurich! O Vienna! Can you be
So psychoanalytically dense
As not to grasp that by considering me
You gain a double health of spirit and sense?

DOROTHEA. I'll never find the man of my desire!

DOROTHY. Then break your heart over a silver birch.

DOROTHEA. But this! No girl could send off such a wire.

DOROTHY. Shock him—or else he'll get you to the church!

33

THE VOLCANIC ISLAND

DOROTHEA. You're right. How often, and with how much pain,
    We burst a lock to find—an empty room!
    But that's all over. Let's be friends again
    And so stay always!

DOROTHY.   Till the crack of doom . .
    And here's *my* gage! Accept the knife I took
    From Borgia (how he'll rail at me, poor ghost!)
    And with it—cut the master's newest book.

DOROTHEA. Where are you going?

DOROTHY.   Going? To the post.

DOROTHEA. Don't hurry. Stop awhile, and take from *me*
    A pledge of golden friendship unalloyed—
    A cup of tea! With milk and sugar?

DOROTHY (*with profound contempt*).   Tea!
    'Oh, for a draught . . .' But here's to Jung!

DOROTHEA (*raising her cup*).   And Freud!

                                       1921.

SQUARE PEGS

Characters
HILDA
A MODERN GIRL
GIOCONDA
A SIXTEENTH-CENTURY VENETIAN

TO H. F. RUBINSTEIN

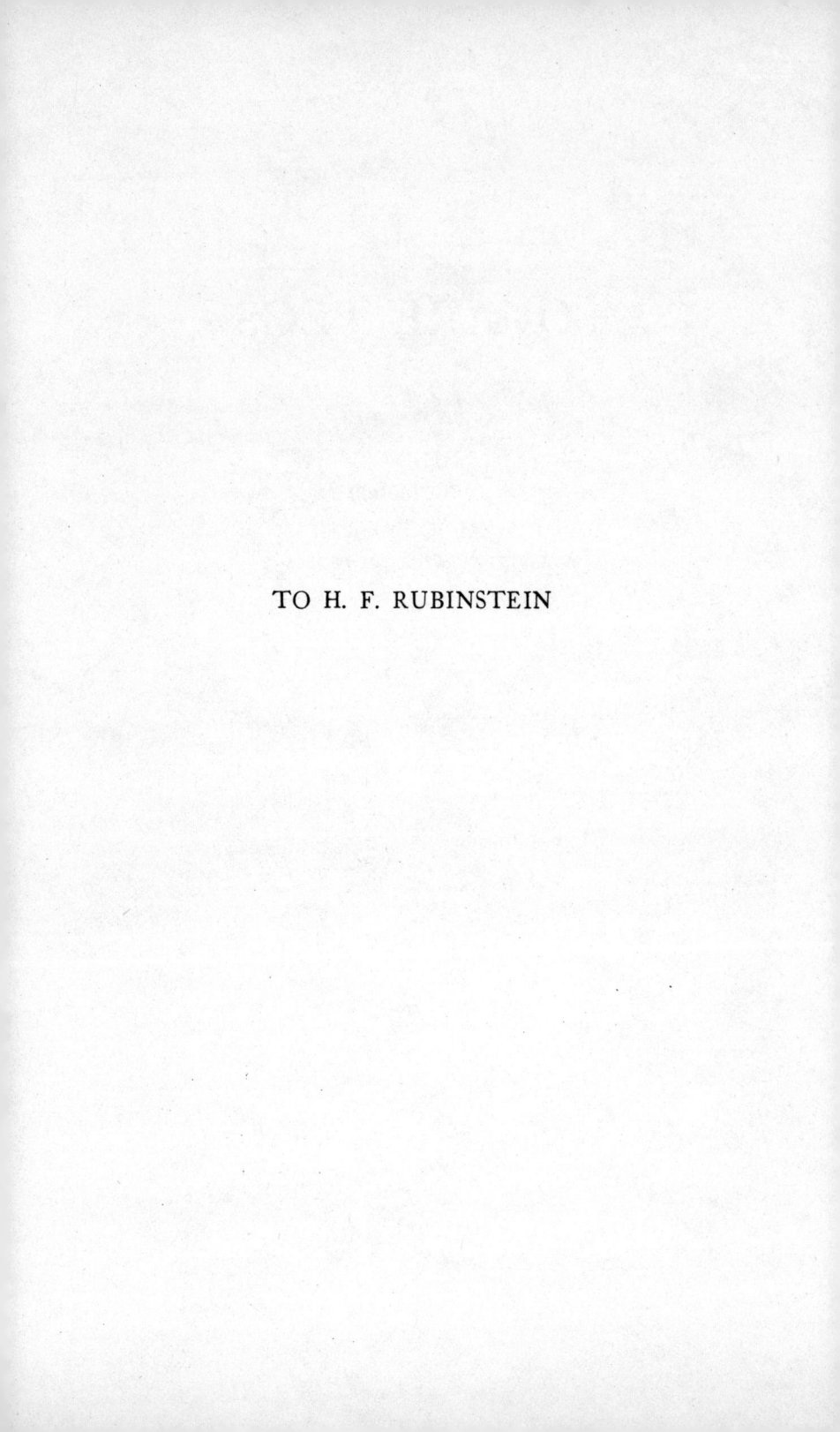

SQUARE PEGS

SCENE. *A Garden. Entrance right and left. Left, a table and two chairs.* (*The general effect should suggest a little lawn which leads outward in several directions.*)

(*The arrival of a taxicab is heard, off. Enter, left,* HILDA *in summer hat and dress and with a light cloak on her arm. She carries a folding-map and a small book.*)

HILDA (*speaking off, left*). What's that? 'The taximeter points,' you say,
  'To fifteen shillings'? Well, didn't I pay
  A pound? What? No, I *haven't* ' made a slip.'
  Surely five shillings was a handsome tip.
        (*Sound of a motor-horn growing fainter.*)
  The creature's gone. These taxi-men! . . . But wait:
  Suppose that isn't really Merlin's Gate,
  Nor this the garden where a girl who loathes
  Our Twentieth Century (all except its clothes)
  May turn the Book of Time to any page
  And move within some more romantic age?
  The map will show. Yes, there's the gate, and there's
  That wall, that table, these two empty chairs . . .
  Everything's right. How wonderful, how splendid,
  To know that here the roar of time has ended!
  Now, let me see . . . (*Consulting her map.*)
            If I should take that road
  What century should I have for my abode?
  'To Ancient Rome.' Lovely! (*She starts to go out, right. Then stops.*)
            It might be serious,
  Though, if I chanced on Nero or Tiberius.
  The Romans were rough diamonds. . . . This way here—
  So the map says—would lead me to the year

Ten-sixty-six. I won't be such a fool
As go back where I stuck so long at school.
William the First was always dull. I know
He'd make me listen to him—standing so,
With Bayeux hands, knee crookèd, and neck bowed—
While he read all the Domesday Book aloud.
I shan't go there. . . . Now, that's a pretty view! (*Referring to the map.*)
'The Eighteenth Century: Boswell Avenue.'
I might try that. But no—that won't do either.
I'd have to wear a wig or tell them why there,
Love coffee-houses more than trees and birds,
And talk in such tremendously long words.
I know, I know! If I can find the way
I'll wander back into the sumptuous day
When, in his gardens near the warm lagoon,
Titian gave feasts under the stars and moon.
That would be heavenly! Those were noble times.
There was a grandeur even about the crimes
Of people like the Borgias . . . and their dresses,
And the sweet way they wore their hair in tresses,
And—oh, and everything! What was Titian's date?
I mustn't err into a time too late;
But how to make quite sure? Suppose I took
My bearings by this little precious book—
Addington Symonds? . . . Oh, that I knew more!
Was it in fifteen-sixty or before?
(*Settling herself in one of the chairs she becomes absorbed in her book. Enter, right,* GIOCONDA *carrying two or three modern novels.*)

GIOCONDA (*speaking off right*). I thank you, gondolier. You drowned my nurse
With true dramatic finish. Take this purse.
So—I am in that Garden where time speeds
Backward or forward as our fancy needs.

SQUARE PEGS

How sick I am of cloaks and ambuscades,
Of poison, daggers, moonlight serenades,
Of those dull dances that are all *I* trace—
Pavane, lavolte, forlana, cinquepace—
And the long pageant of our life at Venice!
Now, in the Twentieth Century there is tennis,
With cream and strawberries round a chestnut-tree,
And day-long idling in the June-blue sea,
And soda-fountains, too, and motor-cars,
And Henley Weeks and Russian Ballet 'stars.'
Oh, what a wealth of joy that century has!
To think that I myself may learn to jazz!
Truly, I judge it has no slightest flaw—
The glorious age of Bennett, Wells, and Shaw.
    (She sets her books on the table and curtsies to them.)
Gramercy, gentlemen,—inasmuch as you,
Here in your works, have taught me what to do,
How to play hockey, smoke, and bob my hair
In nineteen-twenty, when at last I'm there.
Which path would bring me there, I wonder? How
Choose of so many? If I'm near it now
I ought to hear the roaring of their trains,
Their motor-horns, their humming monoplanes . .
    (She listens intently for a moment.)
The very bees are silent . . . *(Seeing* HILDA.*)*
        Who is that?
Surely, unless the books have lied, her hat
Came from renowned 'Roulette's,' in Portman Square!
A Twentieth-Century girl! *She* will know where
The Spaniards gather and the Black Friars dwell.
    (Kissing her hand, right.)
Farewell, Rialto! Bridge of Sighs, farewell!
    (She goes up to HILDA *and curtsies ceremoniously.)*

Dear Signorina . . . Signorina . . . Deep
In Bennett's fragrant works,——or can she sleep?
Could *The Five Towns* have bored her? Let me try
Once more. Most noble Signorina——

HILDA (*starting up*). Why,
Who are you, lady? By your dress and ways
I think you must have come from Titian's days.

GIOCONDA. Indeed, I do. Old Titian! How he talks!
He did my portrait last July in chalks.
But grant me the great liberty, I pray,
Of asking what your name is——

HILDA. Hilda Gray.

GIOCONDA. How sweet and to the point!

HILDA. And yours?

GIOCONDA. Gioconda
Francesca Violante Giulia della Bionda.

HILDA. A poem in itself! The velvet verse
Of Tasso is not softer to rehearse.
What can have led you to forgo an age
When life was an illuminated page
From some superb romance?

GIOCONDA. And what, I wonder,
Can have torn you and your fair time asunder?

HILDA. I'll tell you, for I'm sure you'll sympathize.
I have a lover——

GIOCONDA. That is no surprise.

HILDA. And by the post this morning came a letter——

GIOCONDA. From him?

HILDA. From him.

SQUARE PEGS

GIOCONDA. What could have happened better?

HILDA. Ah! naturally you think that Harry writes
Of longing, suicide, and sleepless nights.
Did he, I'd read his letters ten times over—
But you don't know the Twentieth-Century lover.
Oh, for a man who'd write through tears, all swimmily,
And woo me with grand metaphor and simile!
I couldn't bear the slang that Harry used
In asking for my hand.

GIOCONDA. So you refused!

HILDA. Yes, and came here to seek a braver time.

GIOCONDA. How odd! *I* had a letter, all in rhyme,
Brought by a lackey to my father's gate
Just when dawn broke. As if I couldn't wait!
He dashed up, panting; and his horse's mouth
Was flecked with blood and foam . . .

HILDA (*clasping her hands*). The passionate South!

GIOCONDA. The fellow gave the letter, gasped, went red,
And straightway horse and lackey fell down dead.
I scanned the note, observed the flowery phrases
In which the writer smothered me with praises;
Compared them with the style of Bernard Shaw,
And told him straightway that he might withdraw.

HILDA. If I could see that letter!

GIOCONDA. So you shall,
Sweet friend—or, rather, right you are, old pal.
I'll read it. (*She produces a letter tied with rose-coloured ribbon.*)

HILDA. Do! . . . I see his passion's flood
Demands red ink.

GIOCONDA. Oh dear no—that's his blood.
Now, listen. Did you ever hear a style

Quite so absurd? I call it simply vile.   (*Reading.*)
 'Adored Gioconda—glittering star
   Unsullied by the dusty world,
   Rich rose with leaves but half uncurled,
 New Venus in thy dove-drawn car—
 Have pity: drive thy wrath afar.
   Let Cupid's war-flag be upfurled,
   Lest by thy gentle hand be hurled
 The mortal bolt that leaves no scar.

 'So prays upon his aching knee
   Thy humble vassal, once the fear
 Of Christendom, but now—woe's me!—
   One whose wild prayers Love will not hear,
   Who treads the earth and has no home—
 Giulio Pandolfo, Duke of Rome.'

HILDA. Gioconda, what a lover!

GIOCONDA.   So *I* think—
His brain a dictionary, his blood mere ink.

HILDA. *I* mean how rare a lover! Would that mine
Had brains to pen a letter half so fine!

GIOCONDA. How does he write?

HILDA.   Write! Would you deign to call
 This 'writing'—this illiterate blotted scrawl?   (*Reading.*)
 'Dear Hilda, if you buy *The Star*
   To-night, you mustn't for the world
   Suppose he got my hair uncurled—
 That blighter who kyboshed the car.
 He had the worst of it by far
   Because the hood on mine was furled.
   Good Lord! what steep abuse he hurled!
 Yours, Harry—with a nasty scar.

' P.S.—The cut's above the knee,
    And won't be right just yet, I fear,
      Oh, and what price you marrying me?
        Anything doing? Let me hear.
    Ring up to-morrow, if you're home.
    Where shall we do our bunk? To Rome?

Now, wasn't that enough to make me mad?
It is a shame! It really is too bad!
' Dear Hilda '—plain ' dear! ' And what girl could marry
A man who, when proposing, ends ' yours, Harry? '

GIOCONDA. I love his downright manner. In my mind
I see him, a tall figure; and behind,
His old two-seater. Yes, I see him plainly—
Close-cropped——

HILDA.   Half bald.

GIOCONDA.   Slow-moving——

HILDA.   And ungainly.

GIOCONDA. A brow like H. G. Wells' my fancy draws,
An eye like Bennett's and a beard like Shaw's.
I know your Harry—just the English type,
A silent strong man married to his pipe,
With so few words, except about machines,
That he can never tell you what he means:
But were *I* his, and we two went a-walking,
What should that matter? *I* could do the talking.

HILDA. Surely you see, Gioconda, I require
A lover who can make love with some fire.

GIOCONDA. And I a lover so much overcome
By deep emotion that it leaves him dumb.

HILDA. No poetry? Then, so far as I can tell,
  The Twentieth Century ought to suit you well . .
  I've an idea!

GIOCONDA. What is it?

HILDA. This: that you
  Show me how best you'd like a man to woo.

GIOCONDA. I will, I will!

HILDA. Imagine, then, that I
  Am she for whom you say you'd gladly die.
  This is my room at Baystead: that's the street:
  You must come in from there . . . (*Leading her left.*)
         and then we meet.

GIOCONDA. By Holy Church, a pretty sport to play!
  God shield you, Signorina Hilda Gray! (*Exit left.*)

HILDA. Now—what's the time? It must be half-past four.
  It is. I'll give him just one minute more.
     (*Looking at herself in a pocket-mirror, and making a toilet.*)
  Goodness! I do look horrid. . . . Will he bring
  An emerald or a pearl engagement-ring?
  He comes! I'll take pearls as a last resort.
     (*Enter, left,* GIOCONDA *carrying a pipe and a walking-stick.*)

GIOCONDA. Well, and how *are* you? In the pink, old sport?

HILDA. I'm glad to see you, Harry. Do sit down.

GIOCONDA. 'Some' heat to-day, what? Even here. In town
  Perfectly awful. Got a match?
     (*She tries in vain to light the pipe from a match struck by* HILDA.)
         I say,
  Old thing—you really look top-hole to-day.

HILDA. Well, naturally: I knew that you were coming.
  (GIOCONDA *pulls at her pipe in silence, pokes the floor with her stick, and shifts it from hand to hand.*)
  You're very quiet.
GIOCONDA (*with a start*).   Oh! what's that you're thumbing?
  (*Goes over to* HILDA *and looks over her shoulder.*)
HILDA. Addington Symonds.
GIOCONDA.   Any good?
HILDA.   Why—gorgeous!
  You ought to read it—all about the Borgias.
GIOCONDA. What are they? Oh, I see! I had enough
  Up at the 'Varsity of that sort of stuff.
  I say—oh, blast the thing, this pipe's a dud! (*She puts the pipe on the table.*)
HILDA. You smoke too much. They say it slows the blood,
  And *that* you simply can't afford.   (*Pause.*)
GIOCONDA.   I say——
HILDA. Well, what?
GIOCONDA.   You really look top-hole to-day.
HILDA. How nice! But flattery always was your wont.   (*Pause.*)
GIOCONDA. I say——
HILDA.   That's just it, Harry dear—you don't.
GIOCONDA. I came to ask you something. . . (*Producing a ring.*)
              Ever seen
  A ring like this? Not a bad sort of green.
HILDA (*taking it*). Emeralds! I worship emeralds. They enthrone
  All the luxuriant summer in a stone.
  Do let me just see how it looks! The third
  Finger, I think, is generally preferred?
  How splendid! Won't she be delighted?

GIOCONDA. Who?
HILDA. Your dear Aunt Kate.
GIOCONDA. I bought the thing for you.
HILDA. Harry!
GIOCONDA. *You* know—a what-d'you-call-it ring?
HILDA. Engagement?
GIOCONDA. That's the goods. And in the Spring
The parson gets our guinea. What about it?
HILDA. See, how it fits! I couldn't do without it.
GIOCONDA. Right-o! Then, that's that: good. But if you carry
A diary, jot down, 'Next Spring, marry Harry'—
You might forget. You keep a diary?
HILDA (*bringing a small diary from her bag*). Look—
I did blush—buying an engagement-book!
GIOCONDA. Well, how's the enemy? Good Lord! what a shock!
D'you know, old bean, it's more than five o'clock?
HILDA. You'll have some tea?
GIOCONDA. Can't. Sorry. Told two men
I'd play a foursome with them at 5.10.
You'd better make the fourth.
HILDA. I really can't.
There are some new delphiniums I *must* plant.
GIOCONDA (*going out, left*). See you to-morrow, then.
HILDA. You'll drive me frantic
If you're not just the teeniest bit romantic!
GIOCONDA. It isn't done. You're absolutely wrong
In asking me to do that stunt. So long!
   (*She tosses the pipe and stick off, left.*)
There! Did I play it well? You'd be my wife?

HILDA (*sighing*). My dear, you played old Harry to the life—
His gaucherie . . .
GIOCONDA. His noble self-command . . .
HILDA. The way he shifts his cane from hand to hand . . .
GIOCONDA. A nervous trick that shows how much he feels . . .
HILDA. All I know is—I'd have a man who kneels
And pours out passion in a style as rippling
As the best Swinburne—or at least as Kipling.
GIOCONDA. Then I'll now be *your* lady. To your part—
Woo me as you'd be wooed!
HILDA. With all my heart!
    (*Catching up her cloak, she flings it over her shoulder.*)
Last Miracle of the World, sainted, adored,
Divine Gioconda—hear me, I beg!
GIOCONDA. My lord!
HILDA. Dost know of passion? Is that heart so pure
As not to guess what torments I endure
Who for so long have sighed for thee in vain?
And wilt thou have no pity on my pain?
Wilt thou still spurn me as a thing abhorred
Whose only crime is to love thee?
GIOCONDA. My lord——
HILDA. Stay! I will brook no answer. For thy sake
Did I not paint the town in crimson-lake?
Have I not wrenched thee through thy nunnery-bars?
And bear I not some ninety-seven scars
Taken as I fought my way to thy fair feet?
Think how thy relatives rushed into the street
To save thee—how I put them to the sword
And left them strewn about in heaps!

GIOCONDA.   My lord——

HILDA. Had I a boy's light love when I, to win
  Thy favour, cut off all thy kith and kin?
  Run through the list! Measure my love by that!
  Two great-grandfathers (one, I own, was fat);
  Five brothers; fourteen uncles; half a score
  Of nephews (and I dare say even more);
  A brace of maiden-aunts; a second-cousin;
  And family connections by the dozen.
  Does it not melt that pitiless heart of ice
  To see thyself secured at such a price?

GIOCONDA. My lord——

HILDA.   Or if indeed thy heart requires
  Flame fiercer than my love's Etnaean fires—
  Ask what thou wilt, but do not ask that I
  Live on. Command me, rather, how to die.
  Say in what style thou'dst have me perish here,
  So that at least my ardour win one tear!
  Choose what thou wilt—I'll execute thy charge—
  Nor fear to speak: my repertoire is large.
  I can suspend myself upon a rafter;
  Fall on my blade, and die with horrid laughter;
  Leap from a height; read Bennett's books; or swallow
  Poison—and, mark you, with no sweet to follow.

GIOCONDA. My lord——

HILDA.   Thy choice is made?

GIOCONDA.   My lord——

HILDA.   Alack!

GIOCONDA. I have accepted thee ten minutes back.

HILDA. Then—I will deign to live. My castle stands
  Four-towered among its olive-silvered lands.

Away! Away! Thou art all heaven to me!
   (*She drags* GIOCONDA *right. They break.*)
GIOCONDA. Wonderful! That's Pandolfo to a tee!
HILDA. I should adore him!
GIOCONDA.   And I Harry, too . .
   If only you were I and I were you!
   But soft! since here we stand beyond the range
   Of Time, why don't we swop?
   HILDA.   You mean ' exchange '?
   Why not? We will! (*Moving quickly, right.*)
                      May Titian's age enfold me!
GIOCONDA. Stop! Stop! You can't go yet. You haven't told me
   Where I can find the Twentieth Century.
HILDA (*leading her front, and pointing to the audience*). Then,
   Behold its ladies and its gentlemen.
GIOCONDA. What lovely people! . . . All the same, you know,
   They're not as I have pictured them.
HILDA.   How so?
GIOCONDA. They're all so still. . . . And then—my fancy boggles
   To see not one who's wearing motor-goggles.
   How can I get among them?
HILDA.   You must jump
   Down there.
GIOCONDA.   But that would mean a dreadful bump!
HILDA. You want to go from fifteen-sixty sheer
   To nineteen-twenty. 'Tis a jump, my dear . . .
   And so—farewell! I come, I come at last—
   O fire and sound and perfumes of the Past! (*She goes out quickly, right.*)
GIOCONDA. Her eyes were green. However hard he tries,
   Pandolfo never can resist green eyes.

I know he'll die for her and not for me.
Why did I let her go? It shall not be!
 (HILDA *enters, right.*)
HILDA. It shall not be! Why did I let her go?
Harry will love her more than me, I know.
Gioconda!

GIOCONDA. Hilda!

HILDA. Somehow, after all,
I can't let Harry go beyond recall.
I think of his good heart: I know how proud
I'll be to watch him through a dusty cloud
When his new car, balanced upon one tire,
Rolls roistering through the lanes of Devonshire.

GIOCONDA. I too, fair friend, perceive with sudden terror
The greatness of my momentary error.
I mustn't let you risk the enterprise . . .
Pandolfo never could endure green eyes!

HILDA. Let us each make the best of her own age!

GIOCONDA. But sometimes you will write me—just a page?

HILDA. I will indeed. And you?

GIOCONDA. And so will I.
Hilda—farewell!

HILDA. Gioconda, dear—good-bye!
(*Standing in the middle of the stage, they take hands and kiss. Then they come to the front, left and right.*)
So ends our fantasy—the slight design
 Arisen and gone like sound in summer trees,

GIOCONDA. The burden such as every mind may seize—
That in all centuries life is goodly wine!

SQUARE PEGS

HILDA. Which has the more of joy, her age or mine,
We leave you to determine as you please.

GIOCONDA. Mine has the painting-schools—the Sienese,
Venetian and unchallenged Florentine.

HILDA. Mine has the knowledge that our mortal pains
Are fleeing from the skilled physician's arts.

GIOCONDA. Mine the delight of unspoiled hills and plains,
Fair speech, adventure, and romantic hearts.

HILDA. And mine a sense that, by the single sun
That all men share, the world for man is one.

1920.

Printed at the
CURWEN PRESS
Plaistow, E.13